More Christmas Piano Solos

For All Piano Methods

D0504038

Table of Contents

Book: ISBN 978-1-4234-8362-5
Book/CD: ISBN 978-1-4234-9327-3

7777 W. BLUEMOUND RD. P.O. BOX 13819 MILWAUKEE, WI 53213

Visit Hal Leonard Online at
www.halleonard.com

We Are Santa's Elves

Music and Lyrics by
Johnny Marks
Arranged by Phillip Keveren

Happy March (♩ = 120)

Ho! Ho! Ho!   Ho! Ho! Ho!   We are San - ta's elves

fill - ing San - ta's shelves   with a toy for girl and __ boy, oh,

Accompaniment (Student plays one octave higher than written.) 💿 **TRACKS** 1/2

Happy March (♩ = 120)

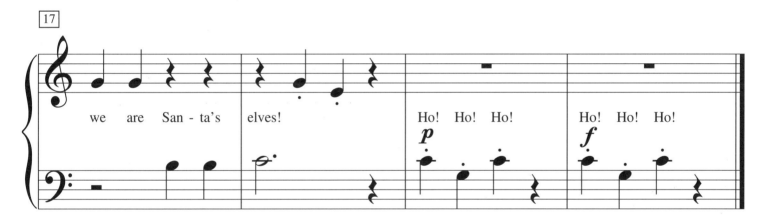

3

Silver Bells
from the Paramount Picture THE LEMON DROP KID

Words and Music by Jay Livingston
and Ray Evans
Arranged by Phillip Keveren

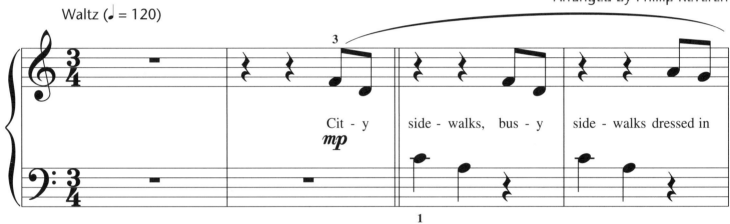

Accompaniment (Student plays one octave higher than written.) TRACKS 3/4

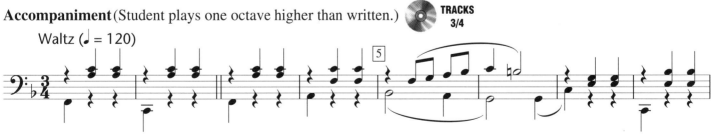

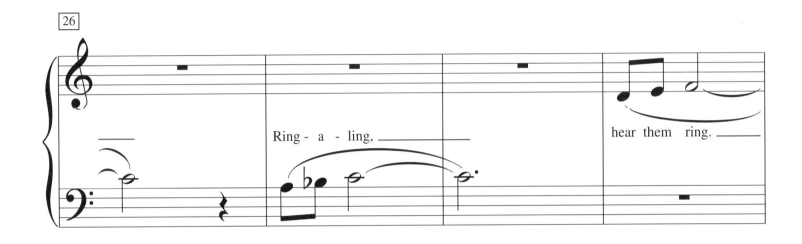

A Holly Jolly Christmas

Music and Lyrics by
Johnny Marks
Arranged by Fred Kern

Moderately bright (♩ = 120)

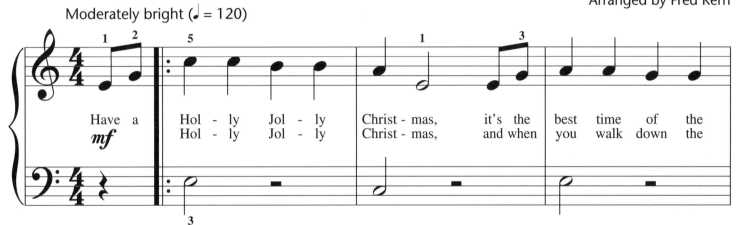

Have a *mf*

Hol - ly Jol - ly
Hol - ly Jol - ly

Christ - mas, it's the
Christ - mas, and when

best time of the
you walk down the

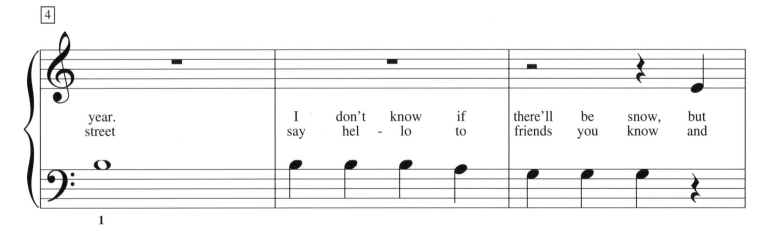

year.
street

I don't know if
say hel - lo to

there'll be snow, but
friends you know and

Accompaniment (Student plays one octave higher than written.) 🔵 **TRACKS 5/6**

Moderately bright (♩ = 120)

mp

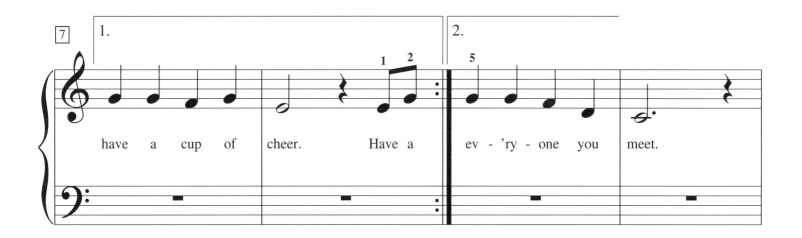

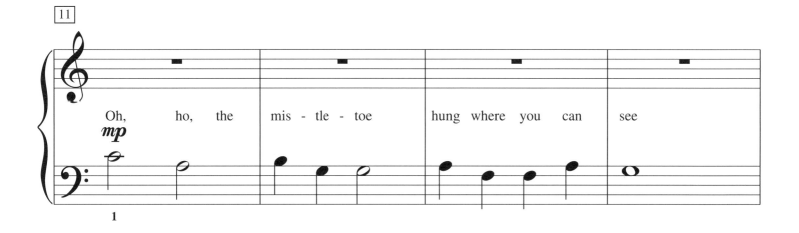

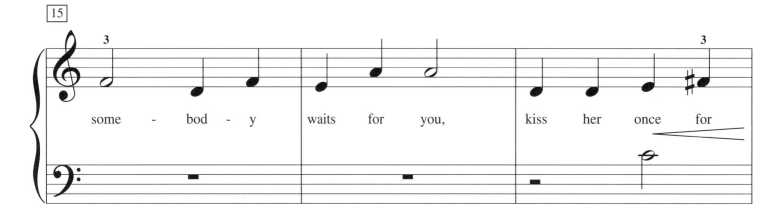

8

me.   Have a   Hol - ly   Jol - ly   Christ - mas,   and in

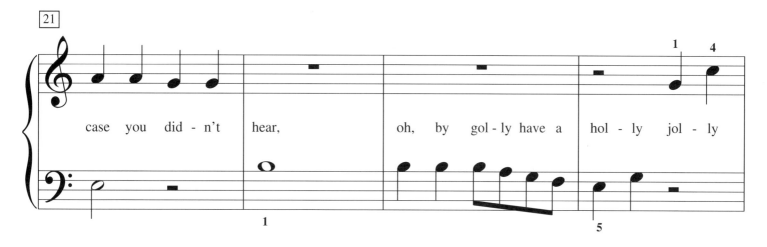

case you did - n't   hear,   oh,   by   gol - ly have a   hol - ly   jol - ly

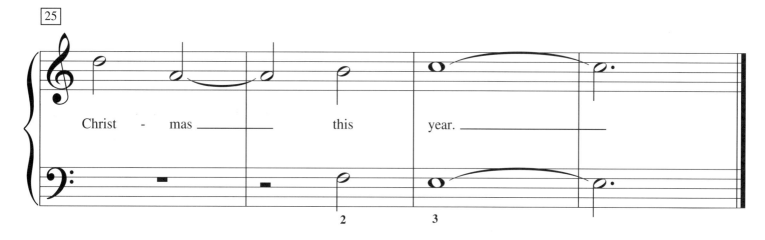

Christ - mas _____________ this   year. _____________

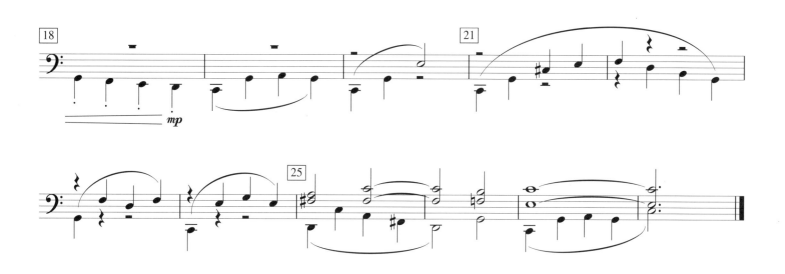

I Want a Hippopotamus for Christmas

(Hippo the Hero)

Words and Music by
John Rox
Arranged by Jennifer Linn

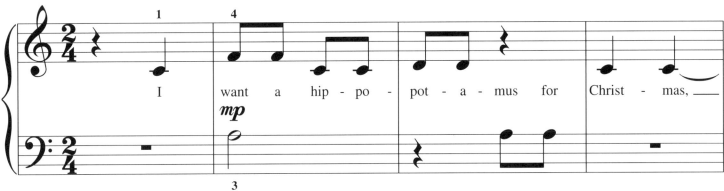

Brightly (♩ = 108) (♫ = ⁝³ ♩♪) swing eighths

I want a hip-po-pot-a-mus for Christ-mas, ___

___ a hip-po-pot-a-mus is all I want. ___

Accompaniment (Student plays one octave higher than written.) **TRACKS** 7/8

Brightly (♩ = 108) (♫ = ⁝³ ♩♪) swing eighths

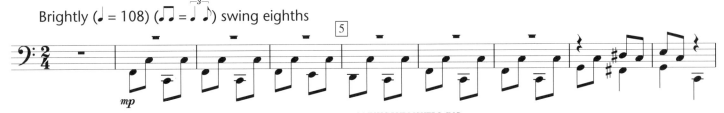

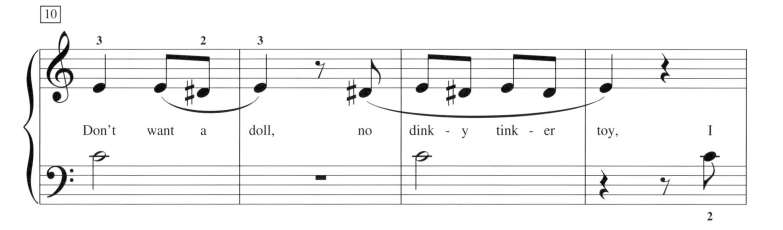

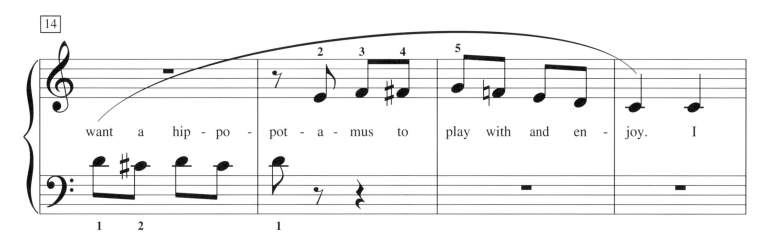

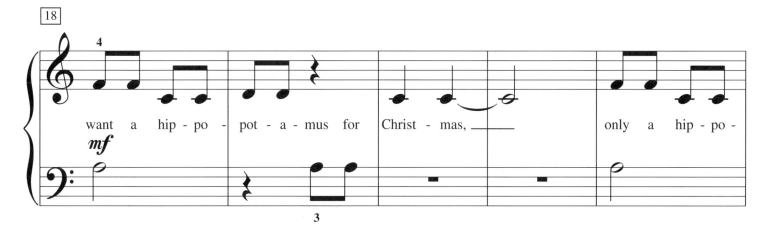

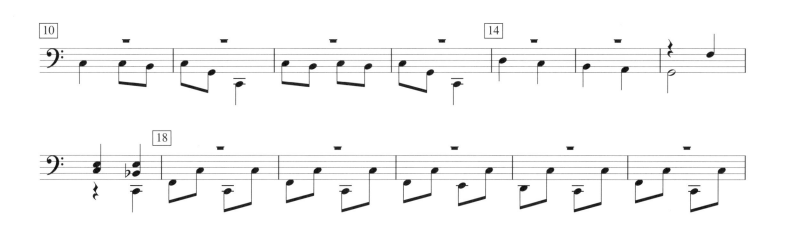

11

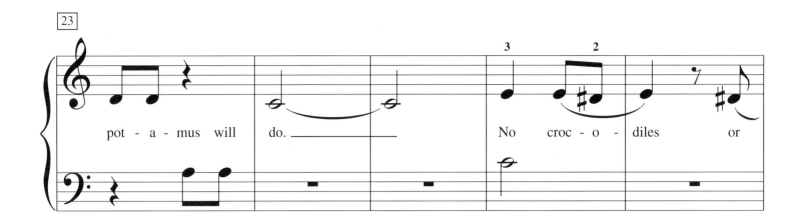

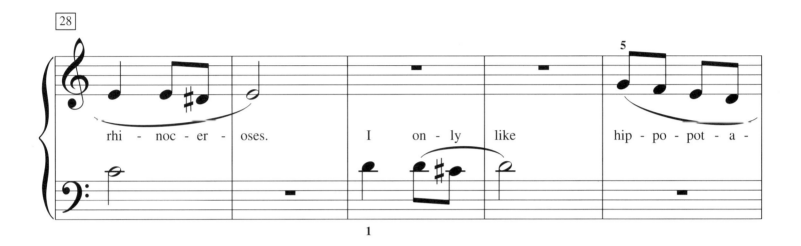

Angels We Have Heard on High

Traditional French Carol
Translated by James Chadwick
Arranged by Carol Klose

Sweetly, with reverence (♩ = 96)

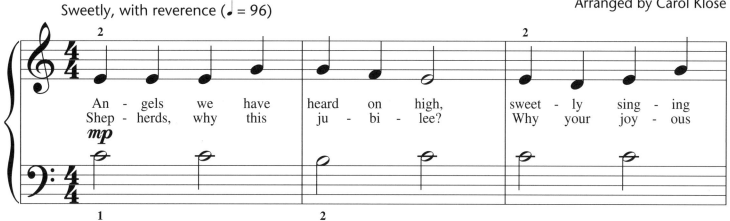

An - gels   we   have   heard   on   high,   sweet - ly   sing - ing
Shep - herds,   why   this   ju - bi - lee?   Why   your   joy - ous

mp

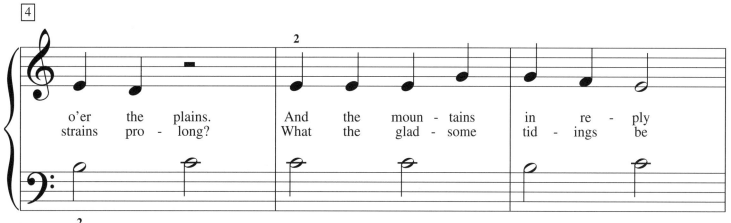

o'er   the   plains.   And   the   moun - tains   in   re - ply
strains   pro - long?   What   the   glad - some   tid - ings   be

Accompaniment (Student plays as written.) TRACKS 9/10

Sweetly, with reverence (♩ = 96)

8va throughout

p flowing
with pedal

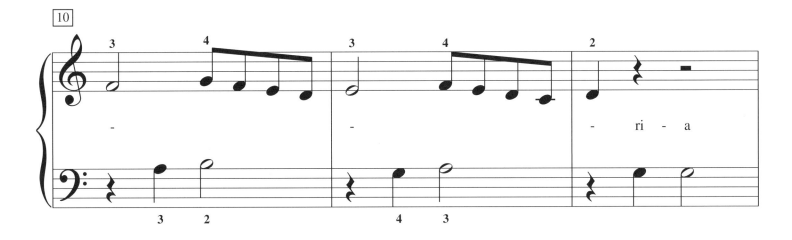

7

ech - o - ing their
which in - spire your

joy - ous strains.
heav'n - ly song?

Glo -

10

- ri - a

7

10

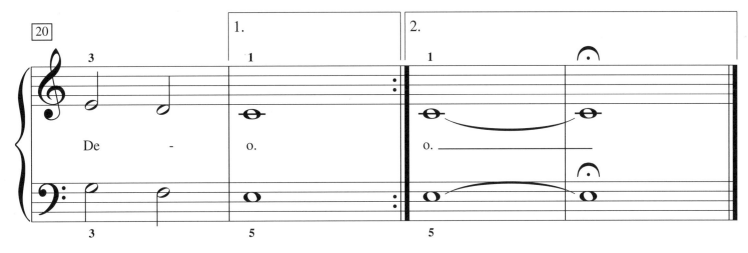

Let It Snow! Let It Snow! Let It Snow!

Words by Sammy Cahn
Music by Jule Styne
Arranged by Carol Klose

With a bounce (♩ = 100) (♪♪ = ♪ ♪) swing eighths

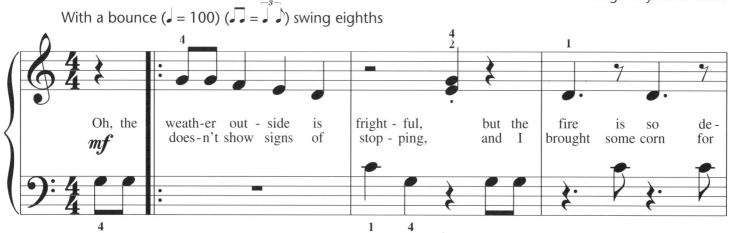

Oh, the weath-er out - side is fright - ful, but the fire is so de-
does-n't show signs of stop - ping, and I brought some corn for

light - ful, and since we've no place to go, let it
pop - ping. The lights are turned way down low, let it

Accompaniment (Student plays one octave higher than written.)

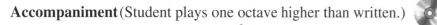 **TRACKS 11/12**

With a bounce (♩ = 100) (♪♪ = ♪ ♪) swing eighths

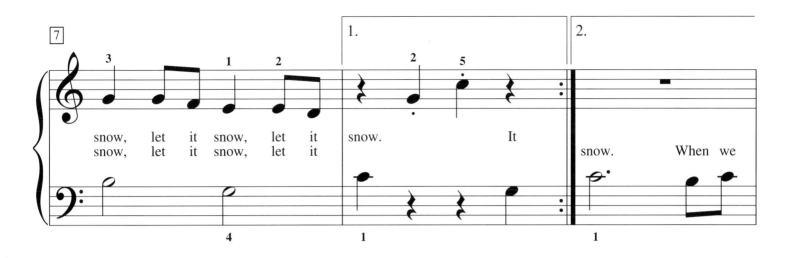

snow, let it snow, let it snow. It
snow, let it snow, let it snow. When we

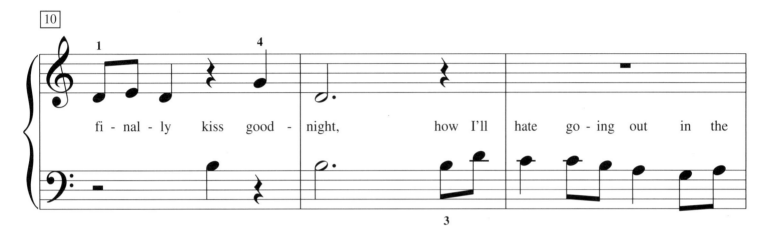

fi - nal - ly kiss good - night, how I'll hate go - ing out in the

storm. But if you real - ly hold me tight, all the way home I'll be

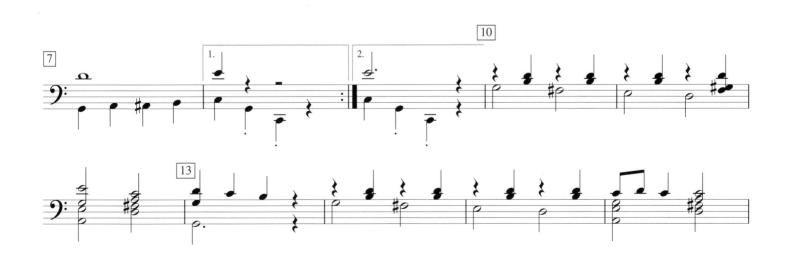

17

warm. The fire is slow - ly dy - ing, and my

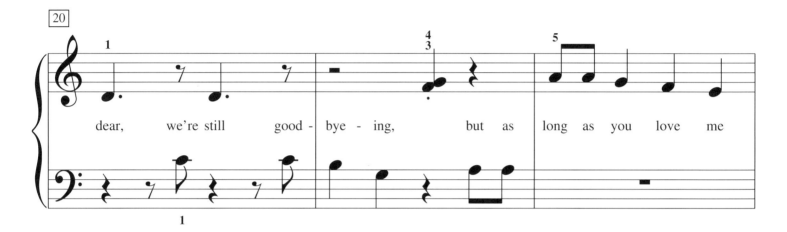

dear, we're still good - bye - ing, but as long as you love me

so, let it snow, let it snow, let it snow.

18

Auld Lang Syne

Words by Robert Burns
Traditional Scottish Melody
Arranged by Fred Kern

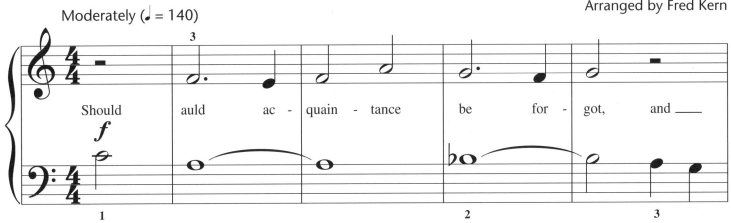

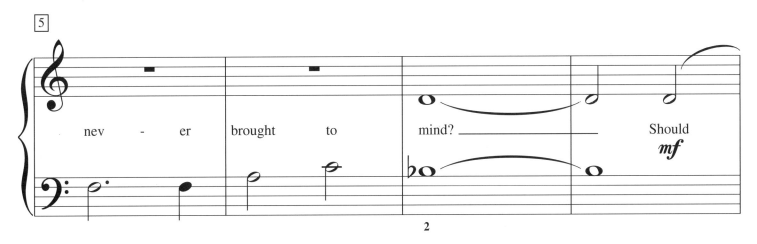

Accompaniment (Student plays one octave higher than written.) 🔘 **TRACKS 13/14**

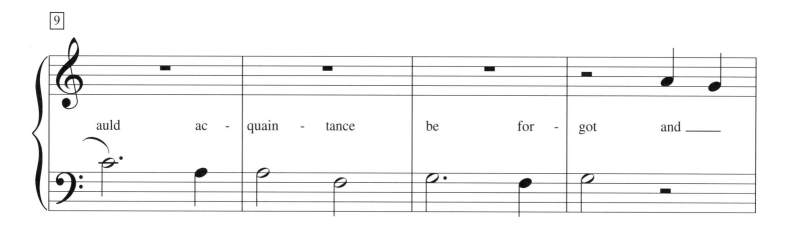

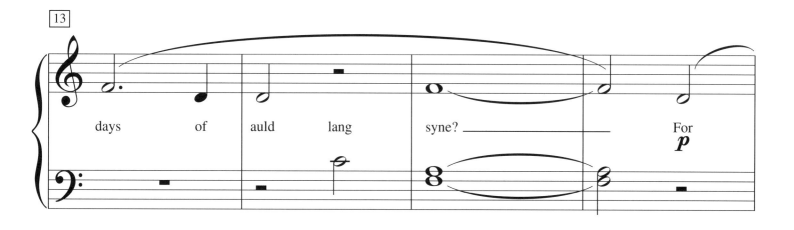

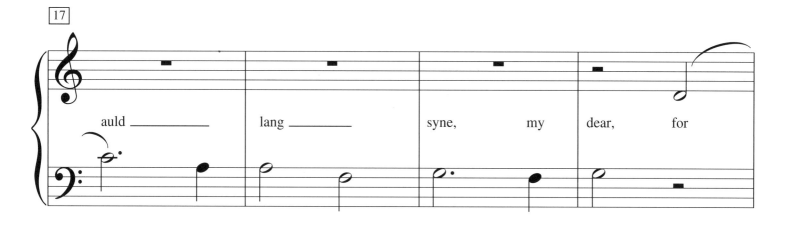

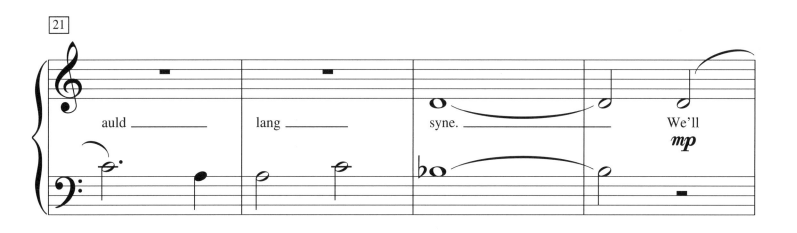

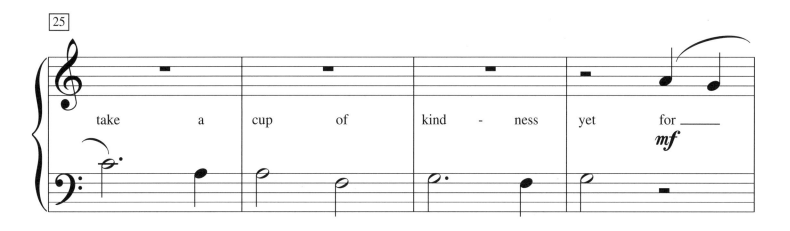

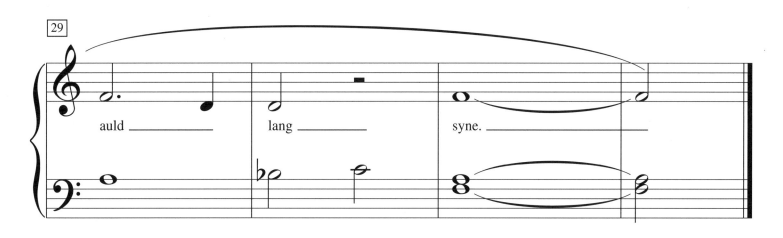

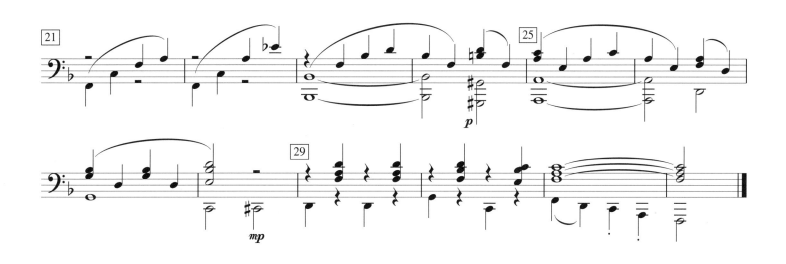

He Is Born, the Holy Child

Traditional French Carol
Arranged by Mona Rejino

Brightly (♩ = 120)

He is born, the ___ ho - ly Child, play the ___ o - boe and

bag - pipes mer - ri - ly. He is born, the ___ ho - ly Child, sing we all of the

Accompaniment (Student plays one octave higher than written.) 🔘 **TRACKS 15/16**

Brightly (♩ = 120)

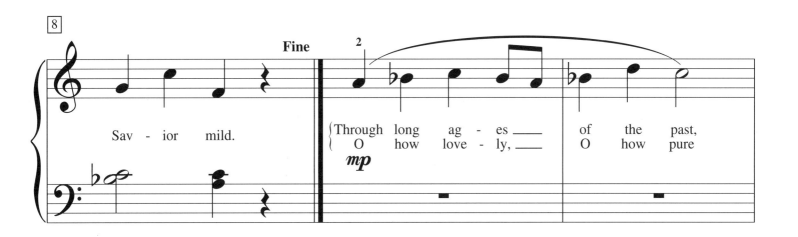

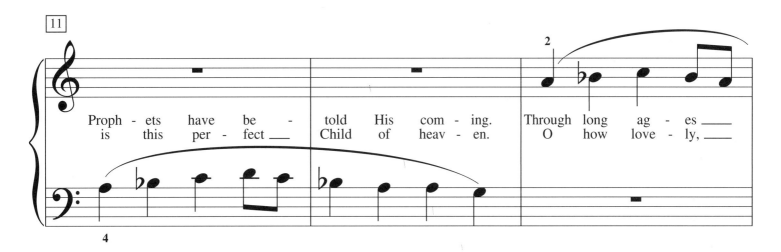

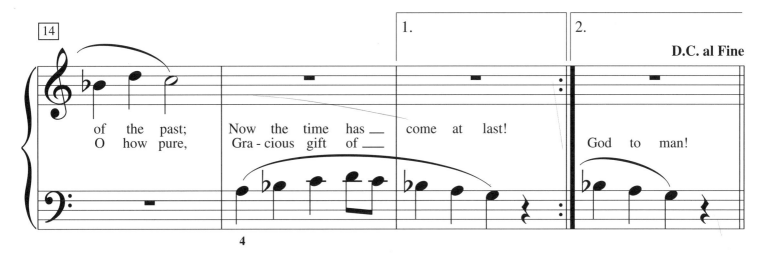

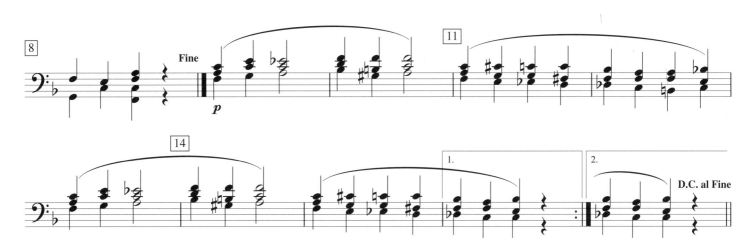

The Twelve Days of Christmas

Traditional English Carol
Arranged by Mona Rejino

Lively; in "two" (♩ = 96) TRACKS 17/18

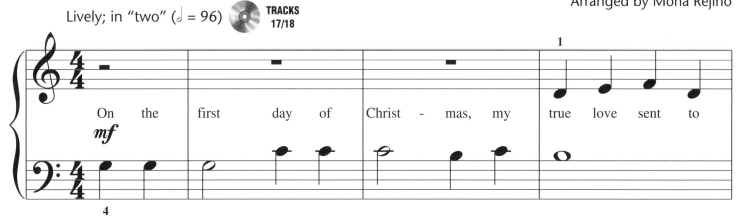

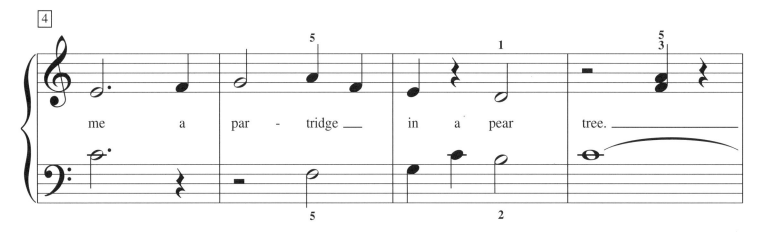

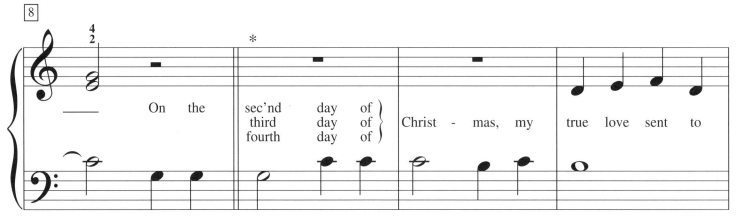

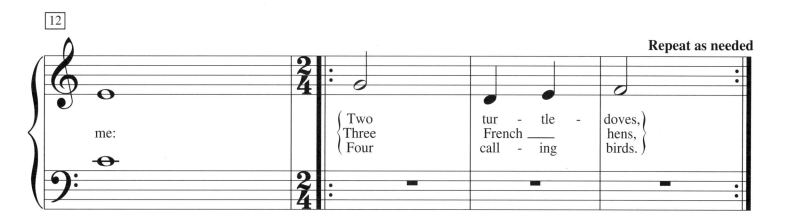

Repeat as needed

me:

Two — tur - tle - doves,
Three — French ___ hens,
Four — call - ing birds.

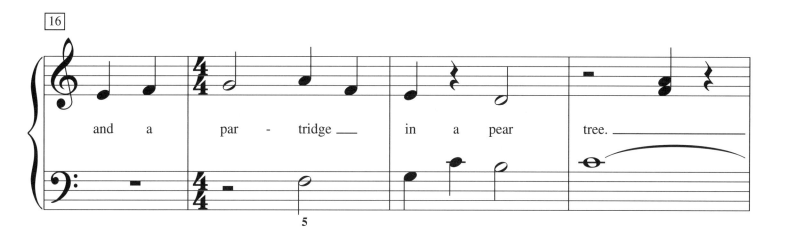

and a par - tridge ___ in a pear tree. _____

5

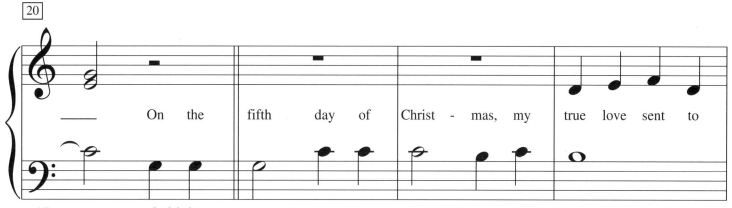

___ On the fifth day of Christ - mas, my true love sent to

*Repeat measures 9–20 for
the 3rd and 4th days.

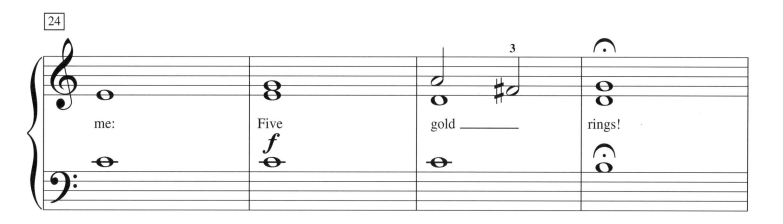

me: Five gold _____ rings!

f

3

25

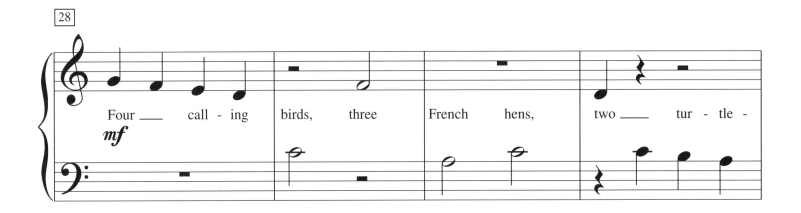

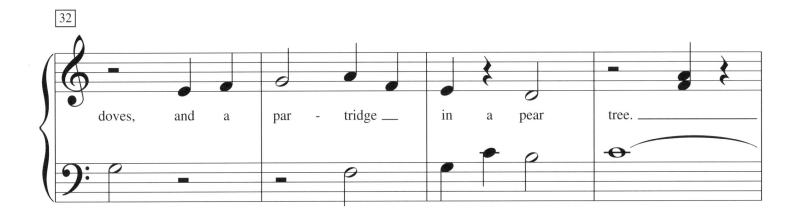

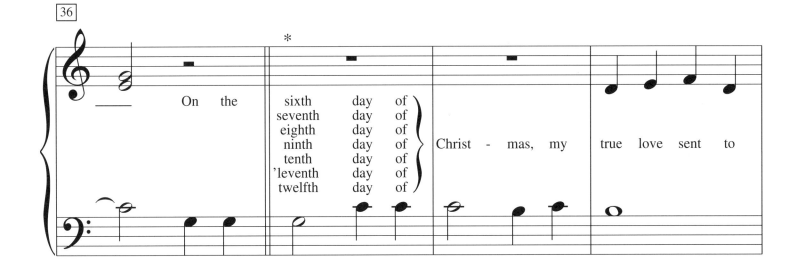

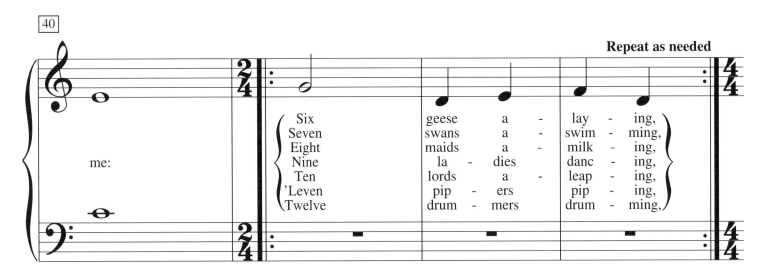

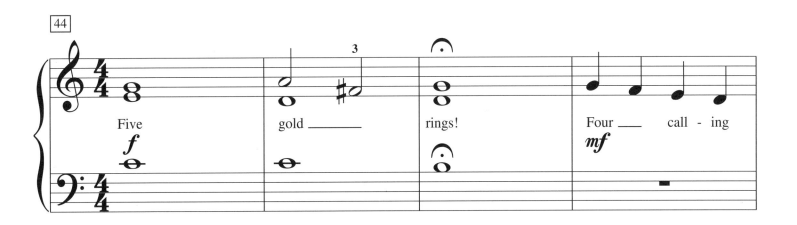

Five gold _____ rings! Four _____ call - ing

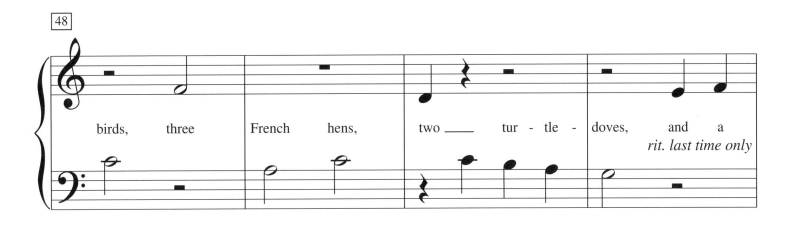

birds, three French hens, two _____ tur - tle - doves, and a

rit. last time only

6th–11th day

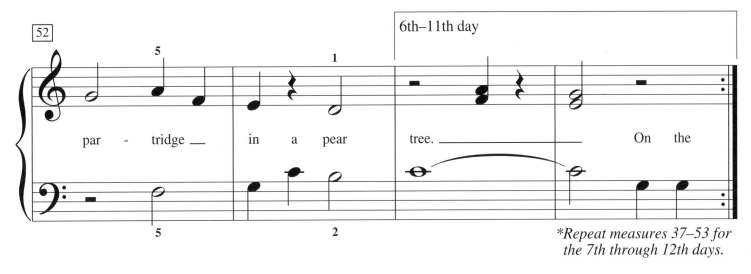

par - tridge _____ in a pear tree. _____ On the

Repeat measures 37–53 for the 7th through 12th days.

12th day

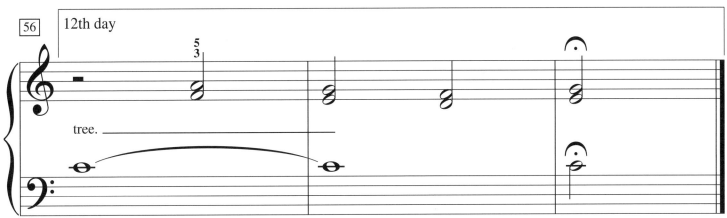

tree. _____

Hallelujah Chorus

from MESSIAH

By George Frideric Handel
Arranged by Fred Kern

Accompaniment (Student plays one octave higher than written.)

TRACKS 19/20

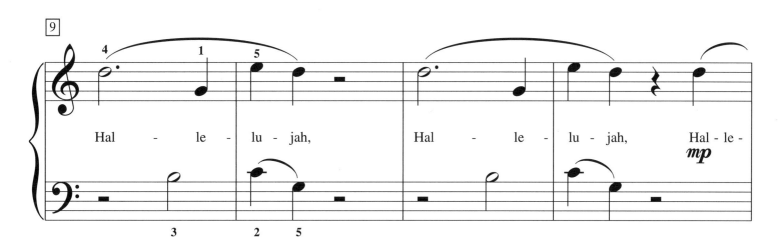

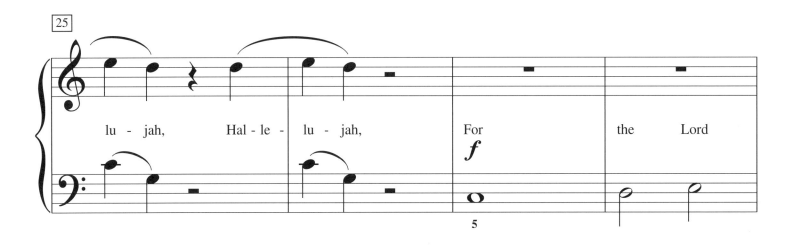

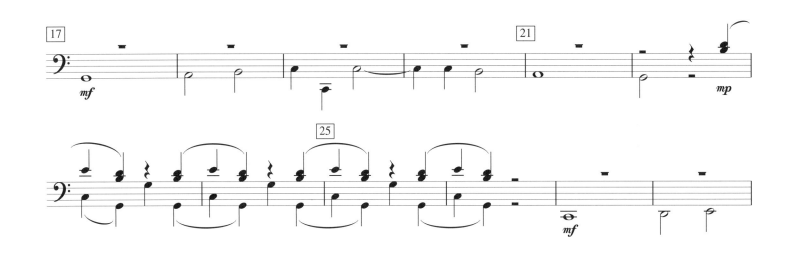

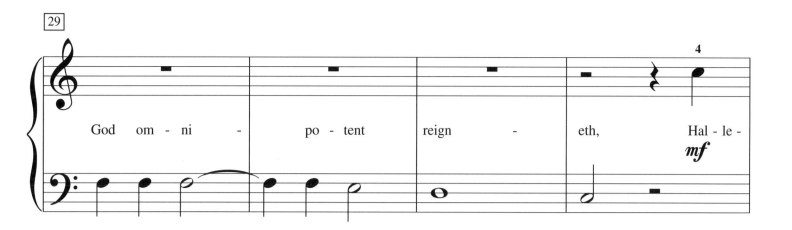

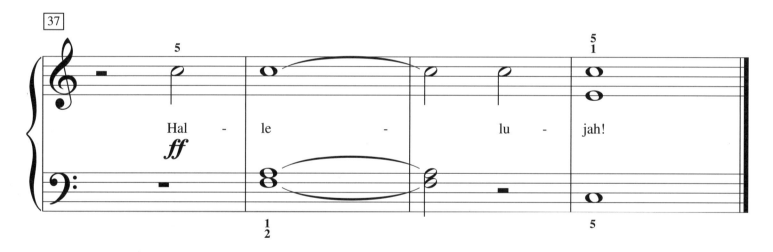

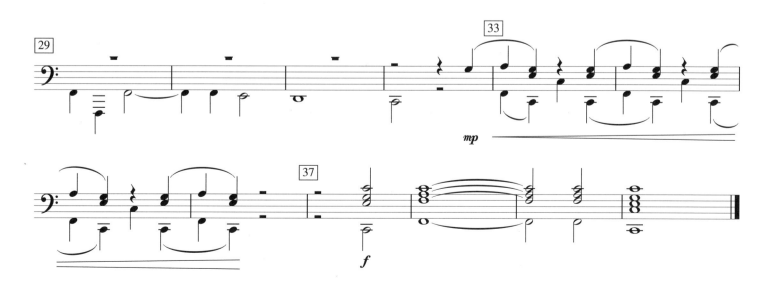

CELEBRATE THE HOLIDAYS WITH THE
HAL LEONARD STUDENT PIANO LIBRARY

Christmas Piano Solos

Favorite carols and seasonal songs, many with great teacher accompaniments! Instrumental accompaniments are also available on CD and GM disk. Arranged by Fred Kern, Phillip Keveren, Mona Rejino and Bruce Berr.

Level 1
00296049	Book Only	$6.99
00296081	CD Only	$10.95
00296101	GM Disk Only	$12.95

Level 2
00296050	Book Only	$6.99
00296082	CD Only	$10.95
00296102	GM Disk Only	$12.95

Level 3
00296051	Book Only	$6.95
00296083	CD Only	$10.95
00296103	GM Disk Only	$12.95

Level 4
00296052	Book Only	$6.95
00296084	CD Only	$10.95
00296104	GM Disk Only	$12.95

Level 5
00296146	Book Only	$6.95
00296159	CD Only	$10.95
00296162	GM Disk Only	$12.95

Christmas Piano Ensembles

Four-part student ensembles arranged for two or more pianos by Phillip Keveren. Featuring favorite Christmas carols and hymns in graded books that correspond directly to the five levels of the Hal Leonard Student Piano Library. CD and GM disk accompaniments are available separately.

Level 1
00296338	Book Only	$6.95
00296343	CD Only	$10.95
00296348	GM Disk Only	$12.95

Level 2
00296339	Book Only	$6.95
00296344	CD Only	$10.95
00296349	GM Disk Only	$12.95

Level 3
00296340	Book Only	$6.95
00296345	CD Only	$10.95
00296350	GM Disk Only	$12.95

Level 4
00296341	Book Only	$6.95
00296346	CD Only	$10.95
00296351	GM Disk Only	$12.95

Level 5
00296342	Book Only	$6.95
00296347	CD Only	$10.95
00296352	GM Disk Only	$12.95

More Christmas Piano Solos

Following up on the success of the Christmas Piano Solos books for levels 1-5 in the Hal Leonard Student Piano Library, these books contain additional holiday selections for each grade level that will work great with any piano method. Each song includes an optional teacher accompaniment. Arranged by Fred Kern, Phillip Keveren, Carol Klose, Jennifer Linn and Mona Rejino.

Pre-Staff
00296790	Book Only	$6.99

Level 1
00296791	Book Only	$6.99

Level 2
00296792	Book Only	$6.99

Level 3
00296793	Book Only	$6.99

Level 4
00296794	Book Only	$7.99

Level 5
00296795	Book Only	$7.99

Festive Chanukah Songs – Level 2
arranged by Bruce Berr

7 solos with teacher accompaniments: Candle Blessings • Chanukah • Come Light The Menorah • Hanérot, Halalu • The Dreydl Song • S'vivon • Ma'oz Tsur.

00296194		$5.95

Festive Songs for the Jewish Holidays – Level 3
arranged by Bruce Berr

11 solos, some with teacher accompaniments: Who Can Retell? • Come Light The Menorah • S'vivon • Ma'oz Tsur • I Have A Little Dreydl • Dayénu • Adir Hu • Eliyahu Hanavi • Chad Gadya • Hatikvah.

00296195		$6.99

FOR MORE INFORMATION, SEE YOUR LOCAL MUSIC DEALER,
OR WRITE TO:

HAL•LEONARD®
CORPORATION
7777 W. BLUEMOUND RD. P.O. BOX 13819 MILWAUKEE, WI 53213

www.halleonard.com

0709